Jarrold Tree Series

With text by **Roland E. Randall**

Trees in Britain

Broadleaved Book 1

Jarrold Colour Publications, Norwich

Many people think of trees as a separate group of plants. In fact a tree is only a woody perennial plant which grows taller and thicker year by year. 'Tree' is really a word of convenience that has no strict botanical meaning. Usually, though, we think of trees as being unbranched for some distance above the ground and as growing to a height of over 20 ft (6–7 m). Shorter plants that are still woody but are branched near the ground are shrubs. However, in good environmental conditions many shrubs will grow to 20 ft (6·5 m) and in harsh conditions some trees will grow only 2–3 in (6–7 cm) above ground level.

The Broadleaved trees are distributed widely among the families of flowering plants that make up our British flora. Some families like the Maples (Aceraceae) include only trees and shrubs; others like the Spurges (Euphorbeaceae) are herbs in Britain but include trees in other parts of the world. Families like the Roses (Rosaceae) include trees, shrubs, and herbs in Britain.

Many plant species include varieties which occur in certain ecological conditions or in certain localities. Some of these can be very difficult to identify. Among the British trees this problem is acute among the Elms (Ulmaceae) and there are other species such as the Willows (*Salix* species) where hybrid forms are common and identification is therefore awkward. Conversely, the trees of each genus are usually very characteristic and identification to that level is easy.

Latin botanical names are included in this booklet because of the precision in description and their international acceptance. The generic name is written first followed by the specific name for example *Fraxinus excelsior*, the Common Ash. This species is in no way related to the Mountain Ash (*Sorbus aucuparia*), which is in fact, a member of the Rose family. After the specific adjective the name (or abbreviation) of the original publisher of the name is given. Sometimes there is a double citation if a later author has transferred the species to another genus. The final information is the maximum height of the species in Britain.

It is a severe problem to know which species to include in a book of British trees. Silver Birch, Scots Pine, Common Oak, Yew, for instance, have been with us since the retreat of the glaciers, whereas Sycamore, Norway Spruce, or Sweet Chestnut are not native, in the sense that centuries ago man introduced them. Those eventually selected for this series are the trees that are more commonly found in town or country outside specialised parks and gardens.

The importance of trees in our landscape is not usually appreciated until they are felled. Both in town and country trees are one of the most significant landscape features. Trees not only add beauty to our landscape but they are also vitally important in creating a suitable environment for other plants and animals. Trees are host plants to many forms of life from mosses and lichens to insects, birds and mammals. Native species like the Oak and the Ash are particularly important in this respect. That is why at a time when new mechanised farming methods are reducing our hedgerows, the Nature Conservancy is encouraging native tree-planting.

This booklet is one in a series which describes trees commonly found in Britain. Here some of the Broadleaved trees are described. The other booklets deal with the Conifers and their allies and further Broadleaved trees.

I would like to thank the following persons or bodies for permission to include photographs of trees on their property: Norfolk Naturalists Trust, Norwich Corporation, Dr E. A. Ellis, Cambridge University, Maurice Mason, Lord Hastings, John Last, and others unknown.

Most of the Broadleaved trees are deciduous, shedding their leaves in winter, though there are exceptions like the Evergreen Oaks and Holly. This means that many other characteristics must be used for identification at other times of the year: bark, buds, flowers, and fruit. Form is rarely of great use for identification because this will vary according to environment. In summer identification is fairly easy because there is usually foliage and either flower or fruit; in autumn the leaves will often be a different colour and ripe fruits may be present; in winter there will only be doubtful form, bark, twig, and bud to assist, but in spring there will be a new flush of leaves often again different in colour and size from the summer crop.

Arrangement of winter buds may be alternate as in Beech, opposite as in Ash or spiral as in Pedunculate Oak. The buds themselves can be many different colours and shapes and may be hairy as Hazel or sticky as Horse Chestnut. The arrangement of leaves follows that of the buds. The leaves may be simple as Birch or compound as Ash and may vary in shape from linear in Willows to triangular as most Poplars. Leaf margins may be entire, wavy, lobed, or toothed, the surface may be hairy or hairless and the colour may vary above and below. Some leaves have long stalks and others are virtually stalkless. Flowers can often help a great deal in naming trees in spring because some Broadleaved trees bear only one sex of flower and others are hermaphrodite. The variety of flower is huge from the catkin of the Willow to the huge spike of the Horse Chestnut. Bark is often a useful characteristic, but it must be remembered that most species have a thin, green, smooth bark when they are young and only attain their typical bark at maturity. Trees like Beech retain their smooth bark for life, but Elm becomes deeply furrowed and Oak becomes cubed. The colour of some barks is often the result of lichens growing on them and this can easily confuse.

The families described in this booklet are Birch, Hazel, Beech, and Willow. All these families bear their flowers in catkins which comprise a main stalk bearing a group of flowers, almost always of one sex. They are mostly wind-fertilised and this has resulted in the individual flowers being rather plain. The Birch family is a small group of trees and shrubs mainly found in north temperate parts of the world. The fruit is usually a flattened nutlet, which is covered till maturity by a protective scale. The family includes the Birches and Alders. The Hazel family differs from Birch in having solitary, naked male flowers at the base of each catkin-scale and leafy coverings round large nuts. Hornbeam and Hazel are the British species in this family, which only occurs in temperate regions of the Northern Hemisphere. The Beech family is a very important group of tropical and temperate trees which have inconspicuous flowers but characteristic fruits: nuts encircled or enclosed by a woody cup or cover. There are three genera in Britain, the native Oaks and Beech and the introduced Oaks and Sweet Chestnut. Oaks have a large single-seeded nut in a scaly or bristly cup; Beech has a triangular nut enclosed in a 4-lobed spiny husk and Sweet Chestnut a shiny brown nut enclosed in a spiny 2–4-lobed cover. The Willows are a widespread family mainly found in colder regions. In Britain the family includes Willows and Poplars. Trees of this family have separate male and female trees, tiny short-lived seeds and soft light wood.

These four families are thought to contain some of the most advanced trees in evolutionary terms within the British flora, and certainly they represent some of the most successful members of the sylvan community. There are few places in this country where trees exist that do not contain one or more of the species described.

Silver Birch, the 'Lady of the Woods' is a much more beautiful tree than the other Birches because of its white papery bark and the tendency of its feathery twigs to drop at the tips like veils. It has become a common garden and street tree because it casts a light shade allowing other plants to be grown below it (1b). In contrast to the Downy Birch, the young branches are hairless and shiny but covered with greyish-white resin-warts. On young trees the bark is bright golden brown, but with age this becomes white though it remains smooth and peels off in long thin, vertical flakes (1c). In old trees the bark is dark, rugged and irregular. The leaves open from the small winter buds in April and are long-stalked, 1–2·5 in long and tend to be less oval than those of Downy Birch but with a more sharply double-serrated margin (3b). The leaves turn yellow and then pale brown in autumn. Male flowers are produced in late summer but remain immature until the next spring. They form narrow, drooping catkins 1·5–2·5 in long (1a). Female catkins are shorter and more slender and are produced in April/May on short shoots below the male catkins. Small fruits are produced in July, wider winged than those of Downy Birch, in such quantity that the ground around is littered. At the same time the catkin-scales fall. The tree has no heartwood, but in Scandinavia it is used for furniture, veneers, plywood, and broom heads. Birch bark was used for roofing shingles and shoes. British Birch wood is little used commercially, but Birch sap is used in some areas to make wine. Birch makes excellent firewood and is sometimes planted as a nurse-crop for some conifers.

1a

1b

1c

1 SILVER BIRCH, WARTY BIRCH, *Betula pendula* Roth 70 ft

2 DWARF BIRCH, *Betula nana* L. 2–4 ft

3 DOWNY BIRCH, COMMON BIRCH, *Betula pubescens* Ehrh. 60 ft, variable

In mountainous areas of the north-east and Scotland **Dwarf Birch** is occasionally found. It is a small shrub with downy twigs and tiny, rounded, blunt-toothed leaves, 0·5 in across, dark glossy green above and heavily veined below (2). The catkins are erect and tiny, 0·33 in long.

The two tree Birches, **Downy Birch** and Silver Birch are not easy to distinguish because they sometimes grow together and hybridise, producing intermediate forms. Typically, though, the Downy Birch has hairy twigs without prominent warts and the patterns on the bark are more horizontal, also the bark peels easily in horizontal strips. Both species are native and probably came into Britain together as conditions improved after the Ice Ages. Today there is a tendency for Downy Birch to be commoner in the north and west of Britain and in damper localities, such as mountain cliffs or the edges of bogs. In harsh conditions it may grow as a low bush, divided to the base into several separate trunks. The bark is usually brown or a dull silvery grey, and the branches spread or ascend stiffly. The buds are longer and stickier than Silver Birch and the leaves are more wedge-shaped at the base and less pointed at the apex, with smaller serrations along the edge (3a). Frequently the leaf, too, is hairy on the undersurface.

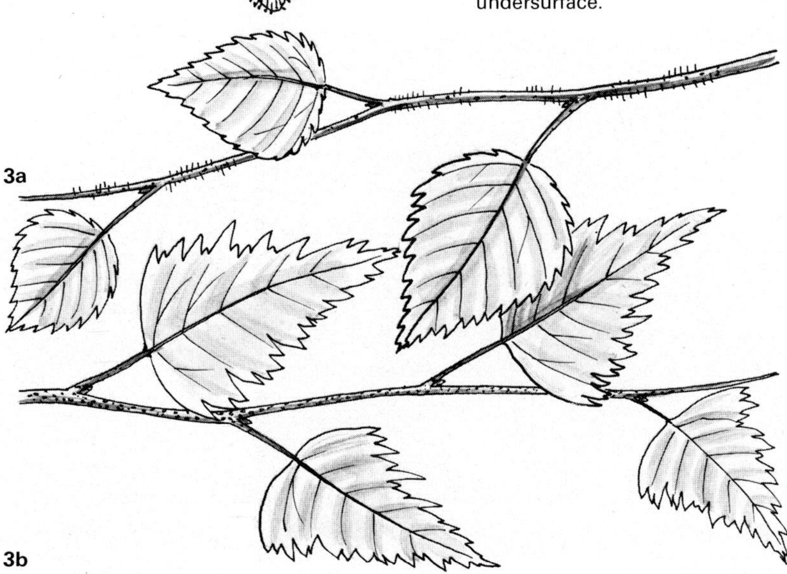

4 ALDER, *Alnus glutinosa* (L.) Gaertn. 70 ft

5 GREY ALDER, *Alnus incana* (L.) Moench. 60 ft

Our native **Alder** develops a distinctive arched crown of crooked branches. It is a tree that is rarely planted, but it will be found commonly beside streams and lakes and can grow in extremely waterlogged soils. In swamps the Alder produces supporting roots from the stem. Flowering begins in March: the male catkins are 2–4 in long and hang down, the female catkins are small about 0·33 in long and upright with red scales covering two tiny flowers. The female catkins overwinter as narrow green cylinders, then thicken during the summer. After the fruit has ripened in October, the catkin-scales become woody and cone-like (4a). Seeds are dispersed the following spring, mainly by water. They remain afloat for about a month buoyed up by corky, air-filled webbing. In early spring three generations of catkins are present on the tree. Alder bark begins smooth, shiny and greenish brown, but with age becomes very rugged and almost black (4b). The leaves open in May and are oval, 2–3 in broad and long, singly serrated, and occur alternately on the twig. Some are dipped at the apex and look as if they are joined the wrong way round. As the leaf unfolds it is slightly sticky, hence the Latin name. The lower surface of the leaf is lighter green than the upper surface and has brown hairs in the angles of the veins. It is one of the few trees on which the leaves remain green until they fall. Alder wood is soft and was once used for clog- and barrel-making; it does not rot underwater and makes good piling and bridge foundations. The timber is white when first cut, but changes to red on seasoning. Today the main use of Alder is for half-round broom heads, toys, and small tool handles. Alder charcoal was once an important constituent of gunpowder. Both Alder and Grey Alder develop nodules on their

4a

4b

Grey Alder   Common Alder Leaf

5

roots in which a fungus lives that enables the roots to make use of free nitrogen in the air. This results in the soils below Alder 'carrs' or woodlands being very fertile. Full-sized Alder trees are rarely seen because they are coppiced regularly.

The **Grey Alder** is a species that was imported from central Europe in 1780 and can be distinguished from our native tree by its hairy annual shoots and buds, its smooth grey bark, stalkless female catkins and pointed, deeply serrated leaves with grey-felted undersurfaces. Each leaf is 2–4 in long and 1·25–2·25 in wide (5). Also Grey Alder reproduces by suckering, and grows on ground that is not so wet as Common Alder. It is often planted especially in towns and as a screen on old coal-tips and is now naturalised in some places. The wood does not season to a red colour as Common Alder and is of inferior quality, but it is sometimes planted commercially to provide protection for other trees against sun and frost. Flowering takes place from early February, but leaves come a little later and the fruits are larger. As with Common Alder the ripening female catkins become woody and resemble small cones (5). These are especially conspicuous in wintertime, hanging in clusters and making identification of the species simple. Both Grey Alder and Common Alder have produced a large number of cut-leaved forms and coloured varieties which are used as garden ornamentals. Many originated wild in Scandinavia.

6 HORNBEAM, *Carpinus betulus* L. 75 ft

7 HAZEL, *Corylus avellana* L. 20 ft+

6a

6b

Birches and Alders are both members of the Birch family but **Hornbeam** is in the Hazel family. The oval crown and smooth grey bark are similar to Beech, but the trunk is deeply fluted and has a metallic sheen (6b). The name 'Hornbeam' means horny or hardwood tree and it is in fact the hardest of our native woods, being used for firewood, wooden cogs, pulleys, and butchers' chopping-blocks, but it is too heavy and dense for most other work and large timbers cannot be produced because of its irregular cross-section. The leaves are alternate and in two rows, pointed, serrated, and very clearly veined, 1–3·5 in long, like a cross between Birch and Elm. The leaves open in May, after Beech, and flowering occurs concurrently. Male and female catkins are cylindrical and pendulous 1·5–2 in long. The fruit is a small nut, 0·25 in long and ribbed lengthwise, partially enclosed by a 3-lobed wing which acts as a sail at dispersal (6a). Hornbeam grows best on low-lying clays in south-east England and is not native in the north. It is an uncommon tree but thought more rare than it is, because of its confusion with Beech. In Kent and Sussex there are large areas of Hornbeam coppice and scrub which were once worked for faggots, firewood, and charcoal. Hornbeam, like Beech, makes a good hedge plant because it withstands cutting and retains its withered leaves over winter, though their colours are less spectacular.

Hazel grows as a many-branched shrub with characteristic brown, peeling, shiny bark that has a large number of light-coloured lenticels (7c). The young shoots are heavily covered with glandular hairs and the leaves are alternate, short-stalked, and rounded, with a diameter of up to 4 in. The leaf-margins are toothed or slightly lobed,

7a

7b

7c

reminiscent of Elm, but they are softer and even at the base. Leaves open in early May and fall in November. Hazel catkins are one of our earliest spring flowers and despite their heavy load of pollen, are often used for decoration (7b). These male catkins form over the summer and mature with the female catkins in February or March. Hazel is frequently unable to fertilise itself and therefore different strains are planted close by. The nuts ripen in August/ September and up to five are clustered together in lobed husks (7a). These nuts are oil-rich and good to eat. Hazel was valued from early times as a rapid native producer of small wood for fences, wattle, and huts and was one of the first woods to be coppiced. Today Hazel wood is of little value and many thousands of acres of Hazel coppices are unused, being replaced by more profitable timber crops, which do not have the lovely ground flora of bluebells, primroses, and violets. Hazel twigs are used for dowsing or water-divining. A cultivated variety with larger nuts is the Filbert. Wild Hazel is an important hedgerow bush over much of Britain, but nuts are often few because of gall-mite infestations.

8a

8b

8c

Beech is one of our best-known trees and occurs in the same family as Sweet Chestnut and the Oaks. It is native to most of England and South Wales, and grows well on the chalk of the Downs and the Chilterns and the soft limestone of the Cotswolds. However, it has been so widely planted that it is found almost everywhere. When grown in the open Beech has a rounded crown. The branches are slender and pendulous and the bark a smooth silver-grey throughout the tree's life (8b). The leaf buds are long and pointed with glossy scales, flower buds are slightly thicker. Leaves develop in late April and are alternate, 1–3 in long with wavy margins. They begin pale green and become deep, glossy green turning bronze, orange, and gold in autumn before falling. Beech makes a good hedge because withered leaves remain till the next spring. Flowers come with the leaves, male catkins being borne in groups of two to three. Each has a drooping tassel of eight to sixteen greenish flowers (8c). Female flowers are in pairs and produce a triangular glossy nut in a woody 4-lobed husk (8a). Good 'mast' years when heavy nut crops occur are irregular. Beech wood is heavy and hard but easily worked and is used for furniture,

8 BEECH, *Fagus sylvatica* L. 100 ft

9 SWEET CHESTNUT, SPANISH CHESTNUT, *Castanea sativa* Mill. 100 ft

9a

9b

9c

turnery, and veneer. Beech woods cast a heavy shade and little can grow beneath them, though their deep leaf litter rots to a very fertile humus.

The **Sweet Chestnut** (9b) bears no relation to the Horse Chestnut other than the similar fruits. However, the spines on the husk of the Sweet Chestnut are more numerous and softer and the nut is more oval and, of course, good to eat (9a). This tree was introduced by the Romans and is now grown as our only economic coppice crop – for cleft-pale fencing. The nuts from British trees are small and only mature in the southern counties; most eating chestnuts are imported from Italy. The leaf is like that of Red Oak but with smaller more regular bristled teeth. In summer it is bright green, turning shiny brown in autumn. Male and female flowers grow on a yellow spike like a pipe-cleaner, with the male flowers at the top. Pollination occurs in July and nuts ripen in October. The flowers are more showy than those of most of the Beech family but are unpleasantly scented; also unusually they are insect-pollinated. Sweet Chestnut grows best on dry, sandy soils. It is a large, wide-crowned tree with fissured, grey-brown bark (9c), the fissures often twisting in spirals round the lower trunk.

10 TURKEY OAK, *Quercus cerris* L. 110 ft

11 LUCOMBE OAK, *Quercus×hispanica* Lam. 80 ft

12 CORK OAK, *Quercus suber* L. 50 ft+

10a **10b**

The **Turkey Oak** is a native of southern Europe and western Asia. It is fast-growing and deciduous, with deep, pointed-lobed leaves 5–6 in in length. These persist on the tree much later than those of our native Oaks, and are grey below with a cover of short hairs. The upper surface is dull green. It was introduced to Britain in 1735 where it was cultivated in parks and gardens and has naturalised on acid soils in some places. Despite the straight form and rapid growth of this tree, the wood suffers badly from shrinkage and warping so that it can be used only for firewood. The bark is rough, fissured, and dark grey (10b) and the branches and twigs thicken noticeably where they meet the stem. The twigs are brown, bumpy, and hairy and carry buds with hairy scales. Flowers of both sexes develop in May, male flowers on long, hanging tassels and females on short stalks. The acorns have short, hairy stalks and ripen in the second year. The shallow cup is covered with long, reflexed, narrow scales giving the appearance of being covered with moss (10a). The point of each acorn is depressed in the centre resulting in a small concavity.

The **Lucombe Oak** is a very striking parkland and garden hybrid that resulted from an accidental cross between the Turkey Oak and the Cork Oak. It developed as a seedling in the nursery of a Mr Lucombe in Exeter in 1765, and the parentage has since been confirmed by experimentation. Because the tree is a hybrid the seedlings develop into variable forms, many of which occur in cultivation, including the Fulham Oak. At one extreme they may pass for Cork Oaks; at the other they have the form of Turkey Oaks. Typical specimens have dark green leaves under 5 in long, less deeply lobed than Turkey Oak, with a small point at the tip of each lobe; the underside is white (11). The leaves of Lucombe Oak remain on the tree until February so that the tree is classed as a partial evergreen. However the leaf-scales at the base of the leaf-stalk fall earlier than those of Turkey Oak. The acorns take two years to ripen and the scales of the acorn cup are shorter, broader, and less regular than in Turkey Oak; also the acorn comes to a point at the top. Like the Turkey Oak the side branches tend to thicken as they near the trunk of the tree. In some books this species is referred to as *Q. lucombeana* Holw.

11

Cork Oak is a fully evergreen species that was imported from the Mediterranean in 1699, and is occasionally planted as an ornamental tree. In southern Britain the acorns will ripen and produce seedlings. The major characteristic of this species is the bark that develops on the trunks of full-grown trees (12a). This is thick, soft, and corky, and in the Mediterranean lands it is partially stripped from the trees every few years and used to make bottle corks, coverings for wooden garden furniture, floats, and ornament bases. In many respects the form of leaf and fruit of the Cork Oak is similar to Holm Oak. However, the acorn may ripen in the first year or may take two years and as a rule the leaf is slightly squarer and has less frequent spines along the margins. The acorns may be up to four in a cluster growing on the end of a long thick stalk; at the point of each acorn there is a hairy knob (12b). The Oak genus is found widely in the Northern Hemisphere and in tropical Asia, but does not occur in Africa south of the Sahara. The name *Quercus* was used as early as Roman times to describe the various species of Oaks.

12a **12b**

13 HOLM OAK, EVERGREEN OAK, *Quercus ilex* L. 90 ft

14 PEDUNCULATE OAK, COMMON OAK, *Quercus robur* L. 80 ft+

The **Holm Oak** is an evergreen tree with leaves rather like holly, though spineless. It comes from the Mediterranean area and is planted, and widely naturalised, round our coasts in the south where it acts as shelter from the sea winds. It was introduced to Britain in 1580 and will grow on any soils, but prefers chalk. It also resists atmospheric pollution and makes a good town tree. The Holm Oak develops a broad, dense crown and has grey, scaly bark that in old trees becomes nearly black and divided into small squares (13a). The leaves are usually 1–2 in long but vary greatly in size and shape. They are woolly when young, but with age become shiny green above and felt-grey below. The acorn is short and mostly hidden in the downy cup (13b). It takes two years to ripen.

There are two Oaks native to Britain, the **Pedunculate Oak** (14b) and the Sessile Oak. The former is an abundant tree of clay and loam soils of southern England and the Midlands while the Sessile Oak replaces it on the poorer acid and peaty soils in the north and west. However, the two hybridise and produce intermediate forms so that some trees are impossible to identify. Type specimens of Pedunculate Oak have smooth branchlets with rather blunt buds. The leaves are extremely short-stalked with the leaf-base gathered into a pair of ears round the stalk, side veins running to the hollows between the lobes, and a hairless undersurface. The acorns are blunt-ended and grow on long stalks. The Pendunculate Oak has the greatest girth of any British tree – up to 43 ft. Young trees have smooth, shiny-grey bark, but with age this furrows and becomes rough and rugged (14c). The crown is an open mass of crooked branches that casts a light shade allowing a considerable ground flora. The leaves are not fully out till mid-May and further shoots commonly appear during

13a **13b**

14a

14b

14c

summer. Pedunculate Oak leaves are 2–4 in long with three to ten irregular marginal lobes. Flowers develop in April/ May, male catkins being yellow, hanging clusters 1–1·5 in long and female catkins are upright. The acorns are about 1 in long and ripen in September (14a). The acorn contains two seed-leaves which are bitter and starchy and which, unusually, remain in the soil at germination. Oaks are credited with great longevity, but few exceed 500 years. Reverence was shown to this tree by Greek, Roman, and Druid alike, perhaps because of the strength, durability, and attractiveness of the timber. The heartwood of both Pedunculate and Sessile Oak is very durable and is used as roof shingles, church building timbers, and in the past was the material of which wooden ships were built. Today it is still our commonest native forest crop because of its versatility and adaptability to many soils and its continued use in heavy-duty and quality decorative work. However, it is slow-growing and may well decline in favour of imported conifers in the future. Because it was the major tree of our primeval forests the Oak is attacked by many insect and fungal pests which have developed a relationship with it over the centuries: defoliation by the Oak-roller moth, whitening by Oak mildew, and Oak-apples and marble galls produced by gall-wasp larvae, are all commonly seen. Today one often sees 'stag-headed' Oaks resulting from land-drainage (14d).

14d

15 SESSILE or DURMAST OAK, *Quercus petraea* (Mattuschka) Liebl. 90 ft+
16 RED OAK, *Quercus rubra* L. sec. Duroi (*Q. borealis* Michx.) 100 ft

The **Sessile Oak** is a stout deciduous tree, similar in appearance to the Pedunculate Oak but the main stem tends to grow higher before branching (15a), and the leaves have long stalks but the acorns are virtually stalkless. Lesser differences are that Sessile Oak has hairy branchlets, more pointed acorns and leaves that taper to the base without the ears clasping the stalk as seen on Pedunculate Oak (15b). Leaf-veins rarely run to the hollows between the lobes, and the undersurface of the leaf commonly has brown hairs at the junctions of the veins. Winter buds of Sessile Oak are said to be more pointed in outline and the bud-scales are paler with membranous edges, whereas those of Pedunculate Oak have bud-scales that are a deeper brown all over. The timbers of the two sorts of Oak are very similar and far greater variation is caused by rate of growth than difference of species. A slow-grown Oak, as many are in the harsher conditions of the north and west, produces soft weak wood only suitable for furniture. The bark of the two species is virtually the same and great value was attached to it in the past for producing tannin for leather (15c). Much Oak coppice was grown for this purpose and also as a source of charcoal in the early industrial economy of Britain. Another important use of our Oaks in the past was for 'pannage', the grazing of swine on the acorns in autumn. Oak grows well with many other tree species and many of our woodlands are mixed oakwoods. Often it is raised with Larch or Scots Pine, and Beech is sometimes planted below as Oak

15a

15b

16

reaches maturity. Oak regenerates easily from seed and is often an early tree to invade waste land. In older books this species is referred to as *Q. sessiliflora* Salisb. because of the sessile nature of the flowers and acorns. The name *petraea* comes from the Latin *petra*, a rock, an allusion to the wood's strength and durability. Some authorities have suggested that this species is the only native Oak to Ireland though both occur there commonly now.

Red Oak is not a native tree but was introduced from eastern North America and is the most important species of the Red Oak group, which includes the Pin Oak (*Q. palustris*) and the Scarlet Oak (*Q. coccinea*) which never grow so large. Red Oak is a stout deciduous tree which develops a broad crown with strong branches. The bark remains a smooth grey-green until the tree is quite old. The leaves are 4–10 in long and have seven to eleven pointed, distantly toothed, lobes from which the end of veins project as bristles. The leaves begin yellow, turn green in summer and are a beautiful red in autumn, especially younger trees (16). Flowers develop in May, similar to those of other oaks, but the males may be extremely numerous. The acorns of Red Oak take two years to develop. The first year after pollination they grow to the size of a pea and reach full development in their second year, becoming thicker and longer than native acorns. Where they are attached to the cup they are flat or concave. The wood is porous and only suitable for cheap furniture, but because it grows fast and well on acid and gravelly soils it is being planted for forestry. It is also planted as a
15c scenic and amenity tree.

17 WHITE POPLAR, ABELE, *Populus alba* L. 80 ft+

18 GREY POPLAR, *Populus canescens* (Ait.) Sm. 100 ft

17a 17b 17c

White Poplar (17b) is possibly a native tree, though it may have been imported from Europe in the sixteenth century. It has a southerly distribution and an attractive white bark, white woolly buds and leaves that are grey-white beneath, green above, and quiver in the wind (17a). It has been planted extensively as an ornamental and waterside tree, and near the coast it is often used as a hedge or windbreak against salt-laden winds. Unfortunately it suckers extensively and may form thickets in damp hollows, but is useful where dense shelter is needed. The leavers of suckers and long shoots are palmately lobed (like Maple) while on short shoots they are more oval and almost hairless. Most poplars produce much larger leaves on their suckers, and those of White Poplar may be 6 in long. The leaf-stalks are 1 in long rounded, and woolly. In autumn the foliage sometimes turns a fiery red and adds to the attractiveness of this tree. The male catkins are 2–3 in long, pendent and with crimson anthers (17c). The females are shorter and contain 4 yellow spreading stigma lobes. The trees are of different sexes and male and female are rarely found together so that fertile seed is seldom produced. Most British specimens are female. The best method of propagation is by cuttings or suckers. The bark of mature trees blackens with age and becomes covered with horizontal rows of black lenticels or pores. The wood of White Poplar is of no use commercially. The name 'Abele', commonly used in East Anglia comes from the Dutch 'Abeel' and is often applied to both the White and the Grey Poplar. Trees of this genus are widespread in north temperate regions and were called *Populus* by the Romans.

Grey Poplar is often confused with the White Poplar because it is similar in many characteristics but is almost certainly native and grows much faster and larger (18a). The name 'Grey Poplar' refers to the downy covering on the undersides of the leaves which is much darker in colour than that of White Poplar (18b). This down wears off over the summer so that the crown becomes greener as the season progresses. The major difference between the two species is that the leaves of the suckers and long shoot of Grey Poplar are never palmately lobed but rounded and coarsely toothed, and the short shoot leaves are very smooth. The Grey Poplar has virtually the same southerly range as the White Poplar and because of its great resistance to wind it is most commonly seen as a windbreak tree. It has a more regular, graceful form than the White Poplar, a silvery-grey flecked bark (18c) and a more extensive root system, and is generally thought to be the better ornamental tree. It may become very large and girths of 17 ft have been recorded. Like White Poplar it is unimportant as a timber tree, but it has the reputation of producing as good floor wood as Norway Spruce yet will not burn readily like the resinous conifer. Some taxonomists have considered the Grey Poplar to be a hybrid between the White Poplar and the Aspen – a hybrid that is sometimes recorded. However, although it shares some of the characteristics of the two species, in other respects it is recognisably distinct and breeds true.

18a

18b

18c

19a

19b

19c

The **Aspen** is the only native species of Poplar that is found throughout the country, and is quickly recognised in summer by the constant fluttering motion of the leaves. Aspen leaves are nearly round, but variable in size from only 0·5 in to over 4 in across and are more heart-shaped on sucker shoots. They are dark green on both sides with a deeply but bluntly toothed, wavy margin (19a). In autumn the leaves turn golden yellow, red, and purple before falling. The leaf-stalks are very long and flattened, though shorter on suckers. The Aspen is a rather slender tree that may be either pyramidal or weeping in form and it varies widely in date of leafing, and quantity of hair on the young leaf. The bark is white- to yellow-grey when young but becomes dark and rugged with age (19b). A useful characteristic of identification is the swollen, corky protrusions on the bark where old branches have been lost. Like all Poplars, the Aspen has separate male and female trees and the flowers grow in long, hanging catkins (19c). The male catkins are up to 4 in long with purple-red anthers, and resemble caterpillars. The females are shorter and contain a round ovary with a 4-lobed stigma. The fruits contain numerous tiny seeds covered with cottony down that aids wind dispersal. If they do not germinate quickly, the seeds perish. Aspen is one of the oldest trees of Britain that probably followed the Birches and Willows into the country as the glaciers retreated. It is a light-demanding tree that stands little competition and is often found in small woodlands and poor heathlands where it grows as a vigorously suckering bush. British Aspen is of little use commercially, though in Scandinavia the white, light, porous wood is used for matches and high-quality paper. There is no heartwood

19 ASPEN, *Populus tremula* L. 80 ft

20 BLACK POPLAR, *Populus nigra* L. 100 ft+

and it makes a useful medium for sculpting. Tradition has it that Christ's cross was made from Aspen wood.

The native **Black Poplar** is found mainly in southern Britain and can be recognised by its deeply fissured black bark with occasional swellings (20c). It is quite a useful timber tree with soft, fibrous wood that does not splinter, but is now uncommon outside the valleys of East Anglia and the Thames because it has been superseded by faster-growing, straighter hybrids (20a). There are two forms of Black Poplar – with and without hairy branchlets, the latter being an introduction from southern Europe. Black Poplars do not sucker extensively like the White Poplar/Aspen group. When grown in the open, this tree has a broad crown and massive down-arching boughs. Shoots begin green but pass through yellow and grey before darkening. The winter buds are oval, red, and pointed, placed irregularly round the twigs. The leaves are dark green, 2–4 in long, and variable in shape but rather triangular though with rounded base angles. The leaf-margin has numerous small teeth and the leaf-stalk is up to $2\frac{1}{2}$ in long and flattened. When the leaf opens it is light brown and it turns yellow before falling. The male catkins, or lamb's-tails open in March before the leaves, 1–2·5 in long with dark red anthers (20b). The females are larger and greenish white. When seed ripens they enlarge to 6 in in length, but the tree is normally propagated by cuttings as fertile seed is uncommon.

21 LOMBARDY POPLAR, *Populus nigra Italica* Duroi. 100 ft

22 BLACK ITALIAN POPLAR, *Populus×canadensis* Moench *serotina* (Hartig) Rend. 120 ft

23 BALM OF GILEAD, *Populus gileadensis,* Rouleau, 60 ft+

Imported poplars are common and the best known of those in Britain is the spire-like **Lombardy Poplar**, which is a mutation of the European Black Poplar which arose in the Po Valley in the eighteenth century and was imported to Britain in 1758. It differs from the typical form only in that all branches rise vertically (21a). The trunk is covered in very rugged dark bark (21c) and is buttressed at the base, often being covered with small branches which bear rather variable leaves (21b). Further up, the bark is smooth and brown. An erect form of the Black Italian Poplar has a similar habit of growth. Nearly all Lombardy Poplars in Britain are male, as they have all been obtained by vegetative propagation. These are preferred because they do not shed the untidy downy seeds. This tree is a handsome landscape species and is widely planted as a barrier against dust, noise, or wind, and when cut down the root system suckers widely. The timber of the Lombardy Poplar is so irregular and full of knots that it is useless even for firewood.

The **Black Italian Poplar** is the commonest of many hybrids that are grown for timber because of fast straight growth. It is a cross between the American *P. deltoides* and Black Poplar, and has been known since the eighteenth century. It is called 'Italian' because it was thought, wrongly, to have arisen there. In fact it developed in France. This species has a wide, fan-shaped crown and deeply fissured grey-

21a

21b

21c

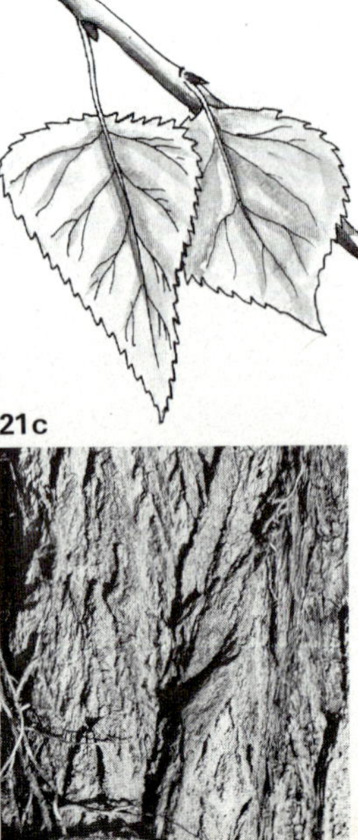

brown bark, free of branches to a considerable height (22a). It is the last Poplar to come into leaf in spring and only male trees are common in cultivation. The leaf is pointed, serrated, and triangular with glands at the base on the leaf-stalk that, in spring, are bronze (22b). It is commonly planted on odd strips of damp, fertile, lowland soils where, within thirty years, it produces large volumes of timber suitable for matches, match-boxes and baskets.

Poplars have often been used in street planting because they grow quickly and tolerate pollution. However, they rapidly get out of hand and draw too much moisture from the soil. **Balm of Gilead** (23a) is one of the worst offenders and when cut down many sucker shoots grow up. This hybrid Poplar has been cultivated since 1755 and is probably a cross between the Balsam Poplar and *P. deltoides*. Old trees have a deeply furrowed stalk (23b). Balm of Gilead has large heart-shaped leaves with white undersurfaces and a hairy leaf-stalk. The buds are large and sticky with scented resin. Flowering takes place in April and May, and the female catkins are up to 6 in long, yellow at first, becoming pink later (23c).

22a

22b

23a

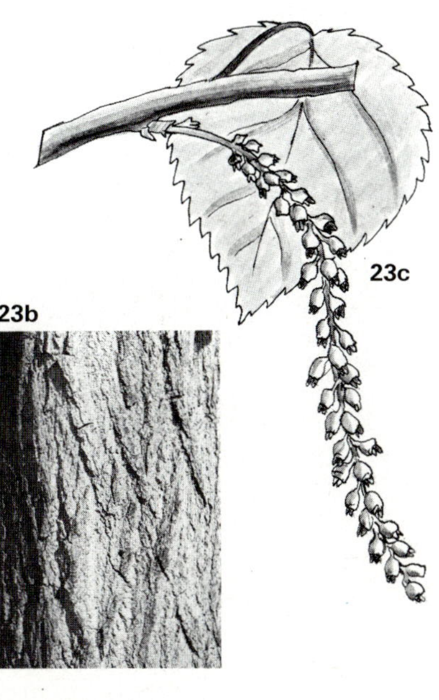

23c

23b

24 BALSAM POPLAR, *Populus tacamahaca* Mill. 90 ft

25 BAY WILLOW, *Salix pentandra* L. 40 ft

24a

24b

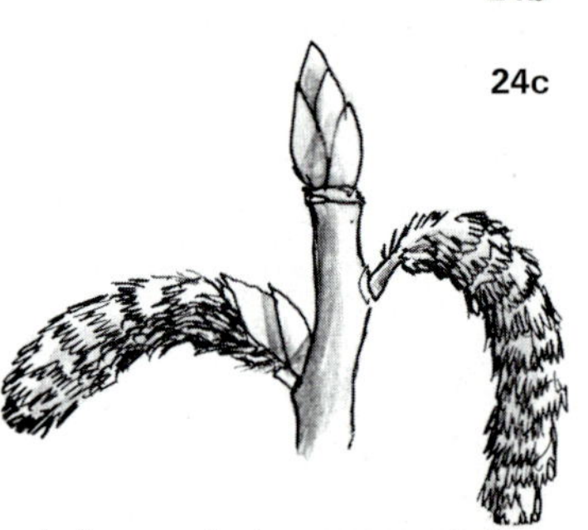

24c

Balsam Poplars have been planted extensively in parks and gardens because of the strong yet pleasant fragrance of their large sticky buds in spring. This comes from the resin which contains an ethereal oil called 'balsam'. Two species are common, the **Balsam Poplar** and the Oregon Balsam Poplar, *P. trichocarpa*. The latter has a silvery leaf which is narrower, and distinctly ridged branchlets. Balsam Poplar has very large heart-shaped leaves, up to 8 in long, with hairy, oval leaf-stalks (24b). In their native North America the Balsam Poplars are important timber-producing trees and they may become useful in the wetter parts of Britain where they grow vigorously, and make excellent windbreaks. The flowers appear in March before those of the Black Poplars and are generally female in Britain. The catkins are yellow, about 4 in long (24c). The bark of this species becomes furrowed when still young (24a). In the past the name *P. balsamifera* was given to both species of Balsam Poplar. Another Poplar occasionally met with is the Berlin Poplar (*P. berolinensis*) which is a hybrid between the Lombardy Poplar and a Balsam Poplar from Asia *P. laurifolia*. Although the branches are erect, it does not have the columnar form of the Lombardy but produces a small crown. It is the only Poplar with both a translucent leaf-margin (as most of the Black Poplars) and a round leaf-stalk (as most of the Balsam Poplars). Mostly it is seen as a windbreak.

Willows are in the same family as Poplars but have entire rather than toothed catkin scales and usually alternate simple leaves. Many of the Willows are dwarf, compact, or creeping shrubs and not described here. The **Bay Willow** is frequent on wet ground

25a

25b

in northern England, and Scotland but rare in the south though often planted. It grows best in fens that are rich in nutrients and on the edges of lakes (25a). It has glossy, olive-brown twigs and buds that look freshly varnished, and dark green, shiny, oval leaves 2–4 in long, with tiny serrations round the margins; the stalk is under 0·5 in long (25c). Although the leaves are like Sweet Bay to look at they have no great fragrance. The tree is leafless for a greater part of the year showing a trunk of greyish fissured bark (25b). The male catkins appear in May/June after the leaves, and are very showy cylinders about 1·5 in long, with yellow-green hairy scales and yellow anthers. The female catkins are green and hairless. The seed capsules open very late and the seeds are dispersed over the winter. As with Poplars, the seeds of Willows must germinate quickly or die. Female Bay Willow trees are very conspicuous when seeds are being dispersed because the seed capsules are covered with a down like cotton-wool to aid dispersal. The timber of Bay Willow is not used commercially.

25c

26 WHITE WILLOW, *Salix alba.* L. 90 ft

27 GOLDEN WILLOW, Salix alba L. var. **vitellina** (L.) Stokes. 45 ft

28 CRACK WILLOW, *Salix fragilis* L. 70 ft

The **White Willow** is one of our two principal timber Willows and is native from Sutherland southwards. The name 'White' refers to the greyish-white colour given to the leaves by a covering of silky hairs. When grown to its full height this is one of our most beautiful trees (26a), but it is frequently pollarded and the long shoots used for rough basketry. The leaves are lance-shaped, 0·5 in wide and up to 4 in long, finely serrated and with glands at the tip of the teeth. The catkins are small and slender, about 1·5 in long (26b). The bark is deeply fissured and grey-brown (26c). White Willow is often confused with Crack Willow, and in fact the two hybridise, but the former is a more graceful tree and the leaves of the latter are greener and virtually hairless, while the branches of White Willow are much more supple. There are several varieties of White Willow, but the major timber species is the variety *coerulea*, the Cricket Bat Willow, which is probably a hybrid between this and Crack Willow. It is the quickest grower of all Willows and may reach 35 ft in ten years on good fertile soil. The wood is very tough and does not splinter and is of course used in the pro-

26a

26c

27

duction of good quality cricket bats. **Golden Willow** is illustrated as one of the common garden varieties of White Willow. It is a conspicuous tree in winter with twigs as orange-yellow as egg-yolks, and broader less hairy foliage than White Willow (27). Frequently this variety is planted as an osier for basket-making.

The second British timber Willow is the **Crack Willow** which is distinguished by the way its small twigs snap away from the branches and its smooth, coarsely serrated leaves which may be up to 6 in long (28a). Timber willows are not normally grown in woodlands but are planted along rivers or on small patches of fertile damp ground. Most of the craft uses of Willow have now died out, but some such as basketry or garden 'trug'-making remain locally. Crack Willow is commonly found in the wild along rivers in the Midlands and the Thames Valley and broken branches are often found, rooted round the parent tree. The bark is coarsely fissured and grey-brown (28b), very similar to White Willow. Roots that grow into the water are red, whereas water roots of White Willow are white. A growth called 'Witches Brooms' often attacks Crack Willow in winter and this may be also found occasionally on White Willow. The catkins of Crack Willow are longer than White Willow, up to 3 in when in fruit, and males are uncommon. There are several varieties, hybrids, and sports of Crack Willow including the Bedford Willow which grows to 90 ft and is rich in tannin, the White Welsh Willow which has yellow twigs, and the Basford Willow, a garden ornamental. At one time about seventy separate native species of Willow were recognised, but now taxonomists have markedly reduced that number.

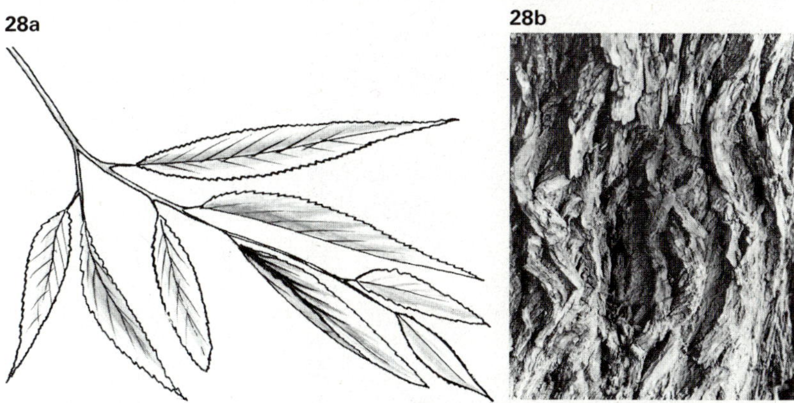

28a

28b

29 ALMOND WILLOW, *Salix triandra* L. 30 ft

30 PURPLE OSIER, *Salix purpurea* L. 15 ft

The most characteristic feature of the **Almond Willow** is the smooth dark grey bark which flakes off in irregular patches to expose a bright, reddish-brown underlayer (29a). It is frequently met with on stream-sides in the lowlands of Britain but is only native in southern localities. The Almond Willow is an exceptionally variable species and is one of the more popular species with basket-makers, who grow it as an osier. There are twenty-two named kinds in cultivation including Black Hollander, Black Maul, Glibskins, and Mottled Spaniards. The wild variety has hairless, lance-shaped leaves 2–4 in long, rather like those of Crack Willow, but finely serrated and with a short leaf-stalk (29b). Some varieties have a bluish tinge and others a glossy green upper surface, and pale undersurface. The cylindrical catkins are erect or ascending and produced during April/May and irregularly throughout the summer. These grow on short, leafy, lateral shoots. The male trees have bright yellow showy catkins 1–2·5 in long; the female catkins are relatively inconspicuous. A variety occasionally found is *hoffmanniana* which only grows to 15 ft and has short male catkins with closely packed flowers. The leaves of this variety are rather small and the same shade of green on both surfaces. Also at the base of the leaf-stalk there are two conspicuous stipules.

Willows for basketry are generally known as osiers from the French word *osière*

29a

29b

30a

30b

meaning a willow bed. The **Purple Osier** is one of the more common of these basket willows. They are usually grown on a coppice system. Planting takes place on well-cultivated arable land near rivers and the osiers are cut back after two years of growth. From the third year the rods can be harvested annually in the spring. Some of the rods are used whole but others are cleft into sections called 'skeins'. Usually the bark is stripped to give the white colour of baskets. In other cases the rods are boiled before stripping, giving a bright buff colour. In olden days every region of the county had its Willow beds and basket-makers, but today the industry is mostly concentrated in Sedgemoor, Somerset. Purple Osiers always grow as a shrub with slender yellow- or purple-tinged twigs and is a native bush locally found on sandy stream-sides. The leaves are hairless, 2–3·5 in long and minutely and irregularly toothed (30a). The apex is acute and the base narrow and rounded. Usually the leaves have a bluish colour but they are very variable in both shape and colour. It differs from all other British Willows in having some leaves opposite, rather than alternate. The catkins appear in late March and April in advance of the leaves. They are small, inconspicuous, and narrowly cylindrical, 0·5–1 in long and almost stalkless, surrounded by a group of scale-leaves. The catkin-scales are oval, hairy, and with purple tips. The male flower has two united stamens with a red-purple anther. The female catkin has an almost spherical ovary and a short-stalked, 2-lobed stigma. In both sexes there is only a single nectary. Young shoots of the Purple Osier are green with pink sheen, but they soon turn a smooth, shining purple. It is a graceful bush, but the bark is very bitter because it contains a large amount of salicin (30b). Thus in some areas it is known as 'Bitter Osier' or 'Bitter Sally'.

The **Common Osier** is a native of central and eastern England, but is more commonly met with as a cultivated bush, though in the wild it may grow to tree-like proportions with pale brown fissured bark, if left uncut. This Osier can be separated from all other British Willows by its narrow, tapering, linear leaves which may be over 10 in in length, dull green above and silver-grey felted underneath (31a). The leaf-margin is wavy and may be sparsely toothed. Twigs and buds are yellow and smooth or finely hairy. Catkins grow in dense terminal clusters in early April before the leaves come out. They are oval, fluffy, about 1 in long with narrow brown scales (31b). The male flower has two stamens and the female a flask-shaped ovary with two stigmas. Numerous varieties of Common Osier are grown including 'Longskins' with a tough peel and 'Brown Merrins' with especially pliable rods. The wood is soft and open grained but makes good hampers and basket staves. Common Osier will hybridise with almost all other British Willows except Bay, Crack, and White, but few people can identify these hybrids with certainty.

To the forester, the **Goat Willow** is a common nuisance of the forest, a tree weed that has to be cut out during the cleaning of the crop because it competes with the planted species, but for most people it bears the handsome 'Palm' blossom which announces spring and which is collected for Easter decoration (32c). Some people call it 'Pussy Willow'. The name 'Goat' Willow indicates that the leaves are a favourite food of domestic goats especially in spring. It is one of the few Willows which is included in the forest community as a small tree. Goat Willow has a smooth or irregularly fissured grey bark (32b) and yellow-green twigs. Catkins buds are a bright, yellow-red and distinctly swollen. The leaves are 2–4 in long and oval or

31a

31b

31 COMMON OSIER, *Salix viminalis* L. 30 ft

32 GOAT WILLOW, PALM, *Salix caprea* L. 30 ft

32a

32b

almost rounded with a dark green upper surface and heavily veined grey undersurface covered with down. The leaf-margin is wavy with irregular teeth and the point is always turned to one side (32a). The fluffy catkins are about 1·5 in long and appear in February/ March well ahead of the leaves. They are virtually stalkless and the males have very long stamens when ripe. The sex of the trees can be told at a distance in spring because the female catkins are silver and the male golden. Goat Willow and Grey Willow are the only willows to reproduce commonly from seed, and both grew up as pioneer species in London after the Blitz. Normally it is common in hedgerows, woodland rides, and as a scrub on waste ground. Some 5,000 acres of Britain are classified as such scrub, mostly in Scotland. The wood is pale cream to pinkish brown but is little used. If cut, Goat Willow coppices vigorously, so that despite the ravages it suffers from man in spring when the catkins are collected it thrives on its persecution. Goat Willow hybridises freely with other Willows. A common imported Willow sometimes becoming an escape is the Violet Willow (*Salix daphnoides*) which is hardy and will grow on drier ground. Its winter twigs are a pleasant violet-brown colour and the silver catkins flower in February/March.

32c

33 GREY WILLOW, COMMON SALLOW, *Salix cinerea* L. 40 ft

34 TEA-LEAVED WILLOW, *Salix phylicifolia* L. 12 ft

33a 33b 34

The **Grey Willow** is the common Willow that is found growing on damp ground all over Britain, but it is not confined entirely to wet situations and may be found growing with Goat Willow. It is variable in form and may be confused both with Goat Willow and the small shrub, *S. aurita*. Sometimes it grows to a fair-sized tree, but usually it is seen as an oblique bush with branches growing at all angles. Willow scrub is virtually impenetrable and is often the pioneer woody growth of fenland. Some taxonomists have divided Grey Willow into two distinct species, *S. cinerea* and *S. atrocinerea*, but they are more likely geographical races of the same species, the former rarely exceeding 15 ft high. The bark is grey and roughly fissured (33b) and the leaves very variable in shape. They are usually somewhat lance-shaped, up to 3·5 in long and irregularly serrated or entire; the short acute apex is twisted (33a). The upper leaf-surface is dark green, but the undersurface is covered with grey felt and sometimes short red hairs. Catkins are similar to those of Goat Willow but are smaller and thinner, and rarely appear before April.

The **Tea-leaved Willow** is described as one of many medium-sized bush Willows that occur with varying frequency particularly in northern England and Scotland. The Tea-leaved Willow is a handsome shrub with shiny brown twigs, glossy buds and rigid, variable leaves 1–3 in long (34). The upper surfaces are a bright, shiny green and retain their colour when dried. The species has a strong tendency to hybridise and there is a continuous series of variations in form, some of which have been regarded as distinct species. In some the leaf is distinctly and regularly toothed. Catkins appear in May with the leaves, and are stalkless (males) or almost stalkless (females) and much more slender that those of Goat Willow. It is commonly found on damp rocks or stream-banks up to 2,500 ft where it may grow as a trailing species. A common bush Willow on siliceous soils in the south as well as the north of Britain is the Eared Willow *S. aurita*, which is rarely over 10 ft high and may be only a spreading shrublet with tiny wrinkled leaves.